Toby and Trish
and the Amazing Book of
Mark

Toby and Trish
(and Boomerang!)
and the Amazing Book of

Mark

by Peggy Hewitt

Illustrated by Tom Hewitt

Text copyright © Peggy Hewitt 1999
Illustrations copyright © Tom Hewitt 1999
The author asserts the moral right to be identified as the author of this work.
Published by **The Bible Reading Fellowship**
Peter's Way, Sandy Lane West
Oxford OX4 5HG
ISBN 1 84101 049 9
First edition 1999
10 9 8 7 6 5 4 3 2 1 0

Acknowledgments
Scripture quotations are taken from the Good News Bible published by
The Bible Societies/HarperCollins Publishers Ltd UK © American Bible
Society, 1966, 1971, 1976, 1992.
A catalogue record for this book is available from the British Library.
Printed and bound in Great Britain by Caledonian Book Manufacturing
International, Glasgow.

Welcome to the Amazing Book of Mark!

Action men

You could never imagine Mark being bored. He was young, full of energy, strictly 'no messing about'. Most important, he knew Peter—that big-hearted, impulsive man who had been a close friend of Jesus. What a pair Mark and Peter must have made!

Mark wrote his account of Jesus' life for the ordinary people of his day, particularly the Romans. Perhaps sometimes he had actually been there. But most of the time Peter told him what had happened. His stories are so real that we feel we are there ourselves. We're actually watching Jesus, the man of action, who had such a powerful effect on Mark's own life.

It's like when you say 'walkies' to Boomerang

The Good News
Mark 1:1-3

This is the Good News about Jesus Christ, the Son of God. (Verse 1)

Have you ever heard somebody trying to start an old car? First of all there's no noise at all from the engine. Nothing seems to be happening. Then it rumbles a bit. Then it rattles. Suddenly, there's a roar. Then it stops and starts a few times until, finally, it settles down to a steady throbbing. All this is called 'revving up', or 'getting going', and when the car moves off you wonder if it will get anywhere at all.

There's no 'revving up', no messing about with Mark. He starts straight away. He's got something important to tell us, and he can't wait to tell it. He's got Good News about someone called Jesus Christ. And there's more to come. Mark tells us that Jesus is no ordinary person. He's the Son of God. Has there ever been such news! Let's keep with Mark and discover what it's all about.

Wait for it...

John the Baptist
Mark 1:4-8

John announced to the people, 'The man who will come after me is much greater than I am. I am not good enough even to bend down and untie his sandals.' (Verse 7)

If the Queen is coming to your town there are people to be told, telephone calls to be made and newspaper announcements to write.

Somebody will come along to make sure that everything is ready. Before we had telephones and newspapers, the official messenger who came on ahead to announce an important event and get everything ready was called a herald.

John the Baptist was a herald and the important event was the coming of Jesus. John knew that he had to do this special job and he lived very simply in the desert so that nothing could distract him from it. Some people felt that John was a great man, but he knew that, compared to Jesus, he wasn't even fit to be his servant. No one but Jesus had God's power to forgive.

3

> He's here, on the same path, in the same river as everybody else!

Jesus is baptized
Mark 1:9-11

Not long afterwards Jesus came from Nazareth in the province of Galilee, and was baptized by John in the Jordan. (Verse 9)

John knew that somewhere in Galilee Jesus was almost ready to start the work he had to do. John didn't know when that would be, or how it would happen, so he just went on with the work *he* had to do until the time came.

Then Jesus came. Quietly he took his place with the crowds waiting to be baptized.

Can you imagine how John felt when Jesus arrived? Nervous, as we feel when our teacher peeps over our shoulder in class? Amazed that Jesus, who didn't need God's forgiveness, had come to be baptized like everyone else? Excited that at last Jesus was beginning his work?

Dear God, help me to do my work for you, knowing that Jesus is near. Amen

8

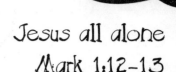

Jesus all alone
Mark 1:12–13

At once the Spirit made him go into the desert… (Verse 12)

After his baptism and the wonderful sign of God's approval, Jesus knew that he had to be by himself to sort things out. He had to go *straight away* somewhere quiet where he could think. Not only to think about what had happened to him by the River Jordan, but also to decide—with God's help—the right thing to do (and how to do it) in the future.

It's not easy for us to find quiet places, even for a little while. But if we do we will find, in the stillness, that we can talk to God and—more important—God can talk to us.

When it goes quiet I can hear you thinking

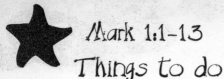

Mark 1:1–13
Things to do

Get-ready exercises for every day

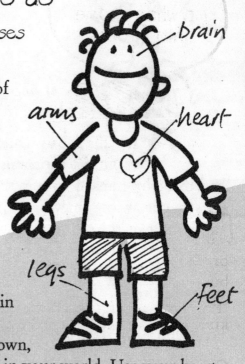

brain

arms

heart

legs

feet

Get the most out of life! Try to keep fit! Don't spend all your spare time playing computer games and watching TV. Use your feet and move around. Use your arms and legs and play some games. Use your brain and find out what's happening in your town, in your country and in your world. Use your heart and read the Bible and get ready to find out about Jesus as you start this amazing adventure.

Toby + Trish — Get ready

Come on, Trish, it's time we were off to the baths

I can't rush— I've got to get ready...

Nobody notices me when I come into a room

Jesus calls four fishermen
Mark 1:16-20

At once they left their nets and went with him. (Verse 18)

There are some people whom, whenever they come into a room, you notice. Not because they're noisy or silly. Just the opposite. They're usually quiet, but they have a lovely smile and there is something special about them. You know they are wise and kind and that they'll be good friends to you.

Jesus was like that. He'd started his teaching in Galilee, but he needed people to help him, to be his friends. Peter, Andrew, James and John had perhaps heard of him, they'd perhaps met him, but when he came to them they didn't need to sit around and talk about it first. They knew straight away what they wanted—to be friends of Jesus. They were ready to leave everything and just trust him.

Lord Jesus, help us to know what we want to do. And then help us to do it—for you. Amen

11

Slamming doors is fine but you've got to open them again to come back

Out of control
Mark 1:21-28

Jesus ordered the spirit, 'Be quiet, and come out of the man!' (Verse 25)

Sometimes when people are very angry they don't know what they're doing. They throw things, slam doors, stamp their feet and shriek. It doesn't seem like them at all.

There are people who are like that all the time—not because they're angry, but because they are ill and can't help it. They can't control what they're doing.

Jesus came along and immediately knew what had to be done. This poor man felt the power of Jesus' love. The peace that Jesus brings came into him so that he became quiet. He became well again and in control of himself, with the help of Jesus.

Jesus heals Simon's wife's mother
Mark 1:29–31

Jesus went to her, took her by the hand, and helped her up. The fever left her, and she began to wait on them. (Verse 31)

Jesus had had a very busy day and he went off to Simon's house with his disciples, probably hoping for something to eat and a chance to rest. Instead, there was no meal ready for them because Simon's wife's mother was ill in bed.

Have you ever been poorly and had to stay in bed for a few days? When you get up you feel strange— your legs are a bit wobbly, like cotton wool, and you soon get tired.

But when Jesus does something he does it completely. Simon's wife's mother must have felt better straight away, because Mark tells us she immediately bustled round and made the meal for everybody—just as though she'd never been ill at all.

The trouble is, when everybody else is asleep, I'm asleep

Jesus gets up early
Mark 1:35-37

Very early the next morning, long before daylight, Jesus got up and left the house. He went out of the town to a lonely place, where he prayed. (Verse 35)

Sometimes if you're very busy or you have a lot to think about, it's difficult to know what to do first—or even what to do at all! It's a question of what is most important.

When the Sabbath day of rest ended at sunset, lots of sick people were brought to Simon's house for Jesus to make them well. This meant that he had to work late into the night. He would probably have liked to stay in bed a bit longer the following morning.

Instead, he was up before it got light because he knew that the most important thing for him was to spend time quietly alone so that he could talk to God. He had little chance of that when everybody was awake, so he used the time when they would all be asleep.

Toby's got
lots of friends
but I'm family

Why Jesus came
Mark 1:38-39

But Jesus answered, 'We must go on to the other villages round here. I have to preach to them also, because that is why I came.' (Verse 38)

If you have a special friend you're sometimes tempted to keep them all to yourself. You like to make plans for them and expect them to do things your way... which isn't always a good idea.

Jesus was staying in Simon's house in Capernaum. Simon liked having Jesus as a guest and thought there was plenty for him to do in the village.

But Jesus had come to teach and to heal as many people as possible, which meant travelling over the whole country. He would never be able to stay in one place for long.

Dear Lord, help me to understand and to share in other people's plans, not just my own. Amen

15

Mark 1:16-39
Things to do
Looking for Jesus

Have you ever met someone famous from TV or films? How exciting! So imagine meeting the Son of God! Make up a little play with your friends in which somebody is always too late to catch Jesus. ('Have you seen the Teacher?' ... 'I'm looking for Jesus.' ... 'Sorry, he was walking on the seashore, but I think he's gone to Capernaum.' ... 'He was in the synagogue, but he's gone to Simon's house.' ... 'He was at Simon's, but he's gone outside the town somewhere—he went at dawn.')

Toby + Trish — That's her

That's her! There she is!

That's not the Queen

The Queen?

I thought we were looking for our head teacher, Mrs Bean

Jesus is certainly worth looking for

The touch of Jesus
Mark 1:40-45

Jesus was filled with pity, and stretched out his hand and touched him. (Verse 41)

Jesus is always able to put himself in somebody else's place and share their feelings.

He knew that because this poor man had a dreadful skin disease nobody would come near him. Not only was he ill, he was dreadfully alone. Try to imagine what that would be like.

The man needed to be healed, but Jesus saw that he wanted something else almost as much. Jesus touched him. The man felt the hand of Jesus on him. Jesus didn't need to touch him. He could have healed him without touching him, but he knew just how important it was for this lonely person to actually feel the nearness of someone else.

Dear Lord Jesus, help me to understand what other people are feeling, and what they are needing. Amen

11

People are coming down through the roof...

Four determined friends
Mark 2:1-12

*Seeing how much faith they had,
Jesus said to the paralysed man,
'My son, your sins are forgiven.' (Verse 5)*

Just imagine. The room is full of people. Jesus is talking, when suddenly there is a noise overhead and a hole appears in the flat roof. Next, a man who is paralysed and cannot move is lowered to the very feet of Jesus. Simon must have been alarmed—it was probably his house and his roof!

But the biggest surprise is yet to come: Jesus forgives the man's sins. Didn't they bring him to be healed? Yes! But first things first! It is important that the things that are wrong on the *inside* of us are sorted out first, then we-on-the-outside can be dealt with.

Now that the man could walk, I hope he would have helped his friends to put the tiles back on Simon's roof!

...and out of the office to follow Jesus

Levi meets Jesus
Mark 2:13-14

As Jesus walked along, he saw a tax collector, Levi son of Alphaeus, sitting in his office. Jesus said to him, 'Follow me.' Levi got up and followed him. (Verse 14)

If anybody from Galilee had looked in at Levi, sitting in his little tax collector's office, they'd have seen a man they didn't like. He was disloyal—he worked for the Romans and took money in taxes which made him quite well off.

When Jesus looked in at Levi he saw a man he wanted as one of his friends. Levi was used to writing and adding up, he knew how to speak foreign languages and he must have been a fairly well-organized person. Levi later became Matthew, one of Jesus' most faithful followers.

We are all different from each other, but when Jesus looks at us he sees what we can become. He loves us for our 'differentness'.

Boomerang looks down his nose all the time

At Levi's house
Mark 2:15-17

Jesus heard them and answered, 'People who are well do not need a doctor, but only those who are sick. I have not come to call respectable people, but outcasts.' (Verse 17)

It's very easy to think you're a bit better than other people. Maybe you live in a bigger house, or you're cleverer at school, or you go to church. It's called 'looking down your nose'. Try doing it and see what you look like. It can stop you seeing things properly.

The Pharisees were like that. They were very religious people and they thought they were OK. So what chance had they of understanding Jesus and why he came?

But Levi's friends knew they were *not* OK— they'd done lots of things they shouldn't have done. What Jesus said was very important to them because they knew they needed God's love and forgiveness.

Something to enjoy
Mark 2:18–20

Jesus answered, 'Do you expect the guests at a wedding party to go without food? Of course not! As long as the bridegroom is with them, they will not do that.' (Verse 19)

Sometimes, when we do the same thing at the same time every day or every week, we do it without thinking. It may be something at home, or at school, or at church. We're like robots.

The people who were fasting were like that. They thought if they went without food they would think more about God, but they did it so often that it was almost meaningless. Even more important, they were so busy trying to please God that they hadn't time to notice that God himself, Jesus, was actually with them.

It was then, and is now, a time to celebrate and enjoy life with Jesus. Jesus wants us to show everyone that life with him is good.

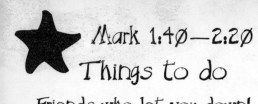

Things to do

Friends who let you down!

Using a large cereal packet, make a model of a square house with a flat roof. Cut a hole in the roof large enough to allow a playdough man to be lowered by cotton fastened to each corner of a stretcher. (Make the stretcher out of the piece you cut from the roof.) How gently can you (and a friend) lower the man through the hole?

Toby + Trish — Fire drill

If there's a fire, you can knot your sheets together and climb out of the window—but it's always better...

...to wait for the fire brigade to arrive

When my shoes crack they let the rain in!

Something new
Mark 2:21-22

'Nor does anyone pour new wine into used wineskins, because the wine will burst the skins, and both the wine and the skins will be ruined. Instead, new wine must be poured into fresh wineskins.' (Verse 22)

Anything new is exciting—like a New Year, particularly if it's a new millennium. If you keep a diary, you have all those blank pages to fill, and New Year resolutions to make—and keep, you hope!

When Jesus lived, wine bottles were made of leather, not plastic or glass. Eventually the old leather dried and cracked and couldn't contain the new harvest of sparkling wine.

Jesus came to make everything new—a new start, a new way of living and loving. The old, 'cracked' religious laws and rules were only necessary until he came: they couldn't contain the 'sparkling' good news of Jesus.

When the tail wags the dog
Mark 2:23-27

And Jesus concluded, 'The Sabbath was made for the good of human beings; they were not made for the Sabbath.' (Verse 27)

Often when something just begins it's good. Then people invent rules and regulations to try to make it even better and before you know it they've forgotten what it was originally all about. They only remember the rules and regulations—they've got it back to front, like 'the tail wagging the dog'.

In Jesus' time, the Pharisees had brought in so many rules that sometimes it seemed that these were what God was all about. Jesus came to show that, most of all, God cares about people and how they are feeling. If they are hungry they must eat, if they are ill they must be made better—even on rest days. But it's good to remember that Sunday is a day when we don't have to be busy and we can use it to think about God and to pray.

Dog wagging tail

When I put my hand up, I'm usually in trouble

Jesus is angry
Mark 3:1-6

Jesus was angry as he looked round at them, but at the same time he felt sorry for them, because they were so stubborn and wrong. Then he said to the man, 'Stretch out your hand.' He stretched it out and it became well again. (Verse 5)

There are lots of very strong feelings described in this story. Peter was probably there when it happened and told Mark about them. Can you pick them out? There are at least five.

This is one of the few times we're told that Jesus was angry, and sometimes it's right for us to feel angry about things that are wrong. But—and this is important—at the same time Jesus felt sorry for these people who had tried for so long to find fault with him. Would they ever learn?

They criticized Jesus for helping others on the Sabbath, the day of rest. But they didn't think it was wrong to go off and plan to kill Jesus on the Sabbath!

A crowd by the lake
Mark 3:7–12

Jesus and his disciples went away to Lake Galilee, and a large crowd followed him... All these people came to Jesus because they heard of the things he was doing. (Verses 7–8)

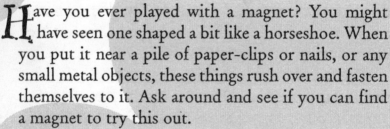

Have you ever played with a magnet? You might have seen one shaped a bit like a horseshoe. When you put it near a pile of paper-clips or nails, or any small metal objects, these things rush over and fasten themselves to it. Ask around and see if you can find a magnet to try this out.

Jesus was just like a magnet. He had a special quality, and when people heard about him they wanted to rush to wherever he was so that they could be near him. They wanted to listen to what he had to say.

Lord Jesus, help us to come close to you and listen to what you have to say to us. Amen

Choosing your friends
Mark 3:13-19

Jesus chose twelve, whom he named apostles. 'I have chosen you to be with me,' he told them. 'I will also send you out to preach.' (Verse 14)

Friends are very important people. They enjoy doing the sort of things we like doing. When we're down in the dumps they can sometimes cheer us up and they would never do anything to hurt us. Most important, we know we can trust them.

Jesus knew how important it was to choose the right people to be his friends because he also had special work for them to do. So he went to the top of a hill where he could talk about it to God in quietness. The twelve people he chose came because they wanted to be his friends.

They weren't perfect. They were just ordinary people. But Jesus knew they would learn from him and eventually be the beginnings of his church.

 Dear God, help me to be a friend of Jesus and to learn from him. Amen

Things to do

In his team!

Just imagine the thrill of being in the team that Jesus set up! And you are! Design a badge for 'The Jesus Team'. Draw it in black and white, colour it in and tape a safety pin to the back.

Pin it to your T-shirt to see how it looks. (If you like, you can send a copy to us at BRF—the address is in the front of the book. We would love to see your ideas.)

Toby + Trish

Our team

How did the World Cup go?

We lost 20-nil, but we were a man short on our team

Who was it, the goalie?

Who is my family?
Mark 3:31-35

'Whoever does what God wants him to do is my brother, my sister, my mother.'
(Verse 35)

Families are very important to us. Not all families are the same 'shape', but they can make us feel wanted and safe. Sometimes we argue and fall out, but if we're sensible, in the end we all sit down together and talk about it. In this way we learn to think about other people and not just ourselves.

Jesus belonged to an ordinary family, which he loved dearly. But he also had another family growing up round him—those people who were beginning to believe he was the Son of God. God is their father, too—and ours—and therefore we are brothers and sisters of Jesus.

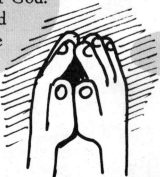

After all, our favourite prayer begins, 'Our Father...'

Finish it quietly in your heart.

29

The sower
Mark 4:1-9

'Listen! Once there was a man who went out to sow corn.' (Verse 3)

When someone says, 'Listen!' just like that, it usually means there's something pretty important coming up. Also, we're expected to use our brains a bit.

Jesus was really into his teaching now, and he had a lot of things to say that were not always easy to understand. So he taught by telling stories which were always about things that the people listening would be familiar with—they were part of their everyday lives. For example, in this story, they would often have seen the sower scattering his seed by hand, and understood his problems with the land.

Jesus' stories are called 'parables'. Notice his little joke, 'Listen, then, if you have ears!' When the seed is grown we call it 'ears' of corn.

The sower—
what it's all about
Mark 4:13-20

'But other people are like the seeds sown in good soil. They hear the message, accept it, and bear fruit: some thirty, some sixty, and some a hundred.' (Verse 20)

In this story Jesus is the sower, his words are the seeds and we are the ground.

Oh those seeds! They went all over the place, because Jesus came for everybody. But some seeds never grew, or they shrivelled up. Not because there was anything wrong with them. The *ground* was the problem—and that means people.

Some people didn't listen at all. They'd rather manage without Jesus. Others listened, but not much. As soon as they had a problem they gave up. A few listened and loved Jesus at first, but there were so many other things to do, or to get, that he soon got squeezed out.

How about us? If we really listen—and pray—then Jesus' words will change us more than we can imagine. In our 'rich soil' his words will help us become how God wants us to be.

A lamp under a bowl
Mark 4:21-23

Jesus continued, 'Does anyone ever bring in a lamp and put it under a bowl or under the bed? Doesn't he put it on the lampstand?' (Verse 21)

Have you ever thought how difficult it would have been to light a lamp in Galilee when Jesus lived there? There was no gas, no electricity and no matches.

It was a long job. First you needed to rub a flint—a very hard stone—on a piece of metal over dry grass or wood until it made a spark. Once you had a fire going, you could keep it burning and light your lamps from it. You could even 'borrow' fire from your friends.

After all that trouble, you wouldn't want to put your lamp where no one could see it, would you?

In the same way, once we know about Jesus, how can we possibly keep him hidden?

 Dear Jesus, thank you that your love shines out for everyone. Amen

I've only got one fault, but I can't remember it!

On a see-saw
Mark 4:24-25

He also said to them, 'Pay attention to what you hear! The same rules you use to judge others will be used by God to judge you—but with even greater severity.' (Verse 24)

Pay attention, Jesus says. Don't let what I am saying go in one ear and straight out of the other. This is important.

Why is it that it's so much easier finding fault with people than praising them? Imagine you're on a see-saw. The lower the person gets at the other end the higher you are at your end. In the same way, pointing out a person's faults can sometimes send them 'down' and us 'up'.

But take care! They say that the faults we find in other people are the very ones we have ourselves and don't know it.

But God knows it. His rules are forgiveness and love. Perhaps we should try to live by those rules and not our own.

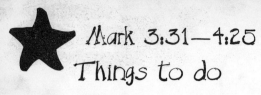

Mark 3:31—4:25
Things to do

Groundwork

Using some card, make a cardboard cut-out sower. Make a field to stand him in and show the four areas: path (and birds), rocks, thorn bushes and good soil. You could do this with real soil, stones and thorny twigs, or make them out of paper and paint with crumpled paper for rocks and thorn bushes. You will have to make and paint cardboard birds either way!

It's not fair! Teacher said I hadn't been listening today

What lesson was it?

Pardon?

Sorry. Did you say something?

A partnership with Jesus
Mark 4:26-29

'The soil itself makes the plants grow and bear fruit; first the tender stalk appears, then the ear, and finally the ear full of corn.' (Verse 28)

Have you ever tried clapping with just one hand? Try it now. What can you hear? Absolutely nothing. Clapping is the result of two hands working together. It's a partnership. Can you think of another example of two things working together? A needle and thread, for instance.

This parable, which only appears in Mark's gospel, is about a partnership between the words of Jesus and our own hearts. If we truly want to be friends of Jesus, then his words (the seed) will root and grow in our hearts (the soil) as naturally as plants grow in a garden.

We blossom into God's people.

The mustard seed
Mark 4:30–34

I keep inventing things but they've all been done!

'It is like this. A man takes a mustard seed, the smallest seed in the world, and plants it in the ground. After a while it grows up and becomes the biggest of all plants. It puts out such large branches that the birds come and make their nests in its shade.' (Verses 31–32)

Awhile ago a man had a tiny idea. Then it began to grow in his mind. Eventually he settled down with wires and wheels and goodness knows what, until he finally sat back and sighed with satisfaction. He'd done it. He'd invented the clockwork radio. He persuaded a factory to produce them and they were shipped to Africa.

Now, even in remote African villages, people can hear what is happening in the world. They no longer feel cut off and alone. All from a tiny idea.

Things grow from small beginnings. From one special person who lived two thousand years ago, the family of God has spread all over the world.

Dear Lord, help me to know that everything I do for you, however small, is important. Amen

The storm on the lake
Mark 4:35-38

Jesus was in the back of the boat, sleeping with his head on a pillow. The disciples woke him up and said, 'Teacher, don't you care that we are about to die?' (Verse 38)

Sometimes things can get a bit on top of us. We might have exams coming up and we're worried. We might be in trouble for something we've done. Or maybe something is happening around us we don't understand. We feel tossed about, up and down, and we're not happy. We stop being able to think straight.

The disciples felt like that. A sudden storm on Lake Galilee was a frightening thing, even for strong fishermen. They were frightened by the waves. They felt lost and alone. Where was Jesus when they needed him?

All right—so he'd had a tough day: he was worn out. But how could he sleep whilst they were fighting for their lives? Didn't he care what was happening to them?

37

28

Jesus quietens the storm
Mark 4:39-41

Then Jesus said to his disciples,
'Why are you frightened?
Have you still no faith?' (Verse 40)

Straight away Jesus saw what needed to be done—and he did it. In a few quiet words he showed that, although he was a man who could get tired, he was also God. That is why he could control the wind and the waves.

Then Jesus dealt with the real problem. After all his patient teaching, he realized that the disciples still didn't trust him fully. He had asked them to take him out in the boat... He had said he wanted them to be his friends and helpers... Would he, after all this, have let them all be drowned while he slept?

The disciples trusted Jesus when things were going well. But when things were hard and they needed him most, that's when they lost their faith. They still didn't understand the power of Jesus.

Lord Jesus, help me to trust you, especially when things seem at their worst. Amen

Teacher forgot to call my name today. I thought I wasn't there!

Who am I?
Mark 5:1-15

And when they came to Jesus, they saw the man who used to have the mob of demons in him. He was sitting there, clothed and in his right mind; and they were all afraid. (Verse 15)

Sometimes we go to the dentist with such bad toothache that he decides to pull the tooth out. Ouch! When the tooth is gone we can see with our own eyes that it was bad and we know that the pain won't come back. The dentist shows us the tooth as proof that it's all over.

The poor man in this story had something far worse than toothache. He was so ill that he didn't know what he was doing or who he was. But he *did* know who Jesus was. And Jesus knew what needed to be done to make the man well again.

When the illness was gone the man could see with his own eyes that it was all over and the pain wouldn't come back. He sat quietly beside his friend Jesus. At last he knew who he was.

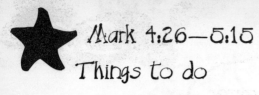

Mark 4:26—5:15

Things to do

Launch the lifeboat

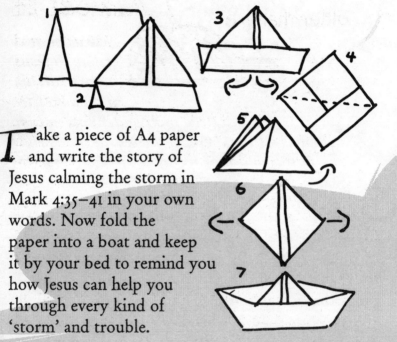

1

2

3

4

5

6

7

Take a piece of A4 paper and write the story of Jesus calming the storm in Mark 4:35–41 in your own words. Now fold the paper into a boat and keep it by your bed to remind you how Jesus can help you through every kind of 'storm' and trouble.

Toby + Trish — Boating

Do you mind taking your hand out of the water?

Why? I'm not splashing you

No. It's making us go round in circles

> Jairus' daughter was only a little older than me

Jairus' faith
Mark 5:21-24

Jairus begged Jesus earnestly, 'My little daughter is very ill. Please come and place your hands on her, so that she will get well and live!' (Verse 23)

Sometimes we don't see things as they really are until we are in danger of losing something precious.

Jairus was not in the habit of throwing himself on the ground and begging people for things. He had an important job in the synagogue and expected to be treated with respect.

But now he didn't care if he made himself look silly in front of a crowd of people. His little daughter was dying. That's what mattered. As he threw himself at Jesus' feet, Jairus knew beyond any doubt that Jesus could make her better. The only thing was that they would have to hurry before it was too late...

I'm holding my breath for Jairus' daughter

Touching Jesus' cloak
Mark 5:25-34

She had heard about Jesus, so she came in the crowd behind him, saying to herself, 'If I just touch his clothes, I will get well.' (Verses 27–28)

If you're in a crowd of people, all moving along, you get jostled and bumped from every side. But nobody really notices you—they're too busy trying to see what's going on.

The woman was different. She didn't just brush against Jesus accidentally. She had a desperate need. She deliberately reached out her hand to touch him. She needed to make proper contact with him. And the moment it happened Jesus knew.

But there was something else she had to do. You can't experience the power of Jesus and keep it all to yourself. It's something to share with others. And as she found the courage to kneel in front of him, she also became aware of his love for her. She was no longer just one of the crowd.

 Jesus, help me to realize that I'm not just one of the crowd. Amen

It's never too late for Jesus

Jairus' daughter
Mark 5:35-43

They laughed at Jesus, so he put them all out, took the child's father and mother and his three disciples, and went into the room where the child was lying. (Verse 40)

Just suppose you have a difficult job to do, or you want to show somebody you can do something special, like a double somersault or icing a cake. The last thing you want is for people to laugh at you and say, 'You'll never do that!' You begin to wonder if you will. It's best to ignore these people and just get on with it.

Jesus had no doubt that he could bring Jairus' daughter back to her parents. But just then these people who were laughing at him would only have got in the way. He had important work to do and he wanted to get on with it.

It's lovely that one of the first things Jesus said when the little girl was walking about was, 'Give her something to eat.'

Thank you, Jesus, that you are always concerned about the ordinary things we need. Amen

43

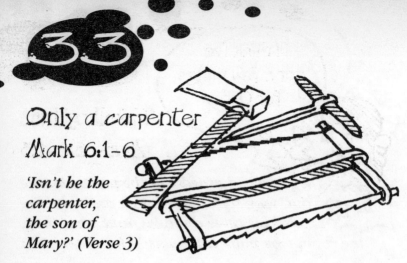

33

Only a carpenter
Mark 6:1-6

'Isn't he the carpenter, the son of Mary?' (Verse 3)

Sometimes if you know somebody very well or have lived with them a long time, they become 'part of the furniture'. You don't see them as they really are. Maybe even jealousy creeps in now and then! Really think about somebody you know well, as though you'd just met them.

'Who does he think he is?' they said. 'He's only a carpenter.' But carpenters can make something beautiful out of something ordinary. They can make old and broken things like new. Just as Jesus was doing with people's lives.

The people of Nazareth wouldn't see this. And because they wouldn't accept Jesus as he really was—the Son of God—they never really knew him at all.

Dear Jesus, help me to know you as you really are. Amen

I think I've got a few things for Oxfam

Travelling light
Mark 6:6-13

Jesus ordered them, 'Don't take anything with you on your journey except a stick—no bread, no beggar's bag, no money in your pockets.' (Verse 8)

Just imagine going off on holiday and not having to do any packing! What difference would it make? You'd maybe do things you'd never done before. You wouldn't be tired and irritable through carrying too much luggage... or worried about losing anything. It would be an *adventure*!

Anything else?

When Jesus sent the disciples out they had nothing—no food, shelter, or, most important, water. A lot of people opened their homes to them—and learned about Jesus at the same time. Because the disciples weren't burdened with too many 'things', they could go further, really get to know people, and concentrate on the work that Jesus had taught them.

Dear Lord Jesus, help us to see that the less 'luggage' we carry around in our lives, the more room there is for you. Amen

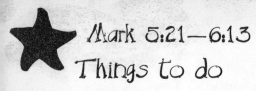

Mark 5:21—6:13
Things to do

Doctor Jesus

Write an interview for the TV news. You knock at the door of Jairus' house and speak to the people who are crying and wailing, to Jairus himself, and then to his daughter (who is just finishing her tea!) Perhaps you could act out your interview with some friends?

Toby + Trish   Sick-poorly

How is your bad cold feeling?

Don't come too close or you'll catch it

I'd quite like to catch three days off school

John in prison—and murdered
Mark 6:19-29

Herod was afraid of John because he knew that John was a good and holy man, and so he kept him safe. He liked to listen to him, even though he became greatly disturbed every time he heard him. (Verse 20)

Have you ever taken part in a tug-of-war? Two teams each take the end of a long thick rope that has a handkerchief tied round it in the middle. The aim is to heave the handkerchief (and the other team!) over to your side. Backwards and forwards it goes until—wallop! It's a real struggle.

Herod had a tug-of-war going on inside him. He knew that John was a good man, yet to please his wife he had John put in prison. But he couldn't help listening when John spoke the truth about him, even though it made him feel awful.

Herod was like the handkerchief in the tug-of-war, pulled between his wife and John... backwards and forwards. Finally, his wife won, because Herod hadn't the courage to do what was right.

47

36

I've NEVER been really hungry

A hungry crowd
Mark 6:3Ø-37

'You yourselves give them something to eat,' Jesus answered. (Verse 37)

It's so easy to live in our own little 'box', just thinking about ourselves, not caring about other people. After all, it might cost us... in time, or effort, or even money, if we did. The girl at school who's lost her book... the boy who's hurt his leg. You can think of a lot more.

We often hear, or even say ourselves, 'It's their own silly fault,' or, 'I'm not getting involved... let someone else do it... it's not my responsibility.'

The disciples were feeling like that. Besides, they were hungry themselves. 'Send the crowd away to get their own food,' they said. But Jesus wanted them to care about other people, even though it meant forgetting themselves. He wants *us* to care about other people, too.

Jesus feeds five thousand people
Mark 6:37-44

Everyone ate and had enough. (Verse 42)

We've all got something we can do best. It may not be very grand like winning a tennis tournament or a painting competition. We may not be very good at maths or roller skating. But there is *something* we're good at. Maybe we're a bit nervous about it and think it won't make any difference to Jesus.

I'm sure the little boy felt like that. Amongst all those people what difference would his picnic make? But Jesus took it and made it into something wonderful when it was given to him.

In the same way, Jesus can transform a smile— your smile—so that it makes a difference to a lot of people. Or an errand—your errand—into something special for a lonely person. Nothing is too small for Jesus to use.

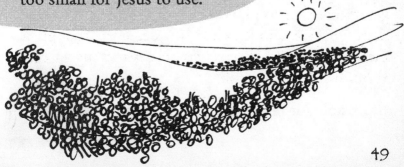

Jesus walks on water
Mark 6:45-52

They were all terrified when they saw him. Jesus spoke to them at once. 'Courage!' he said. 'It is I. Don't be afraid!' (Verse 50)

When something unusual happens we can't always take it in. I was once on a boat, on holiday, when suddenly we were surrounded by dolphins. They leapt and played and we couldn't help feeling wonderfully happy. Then suddenly they were gone. Had they really been there? Have you ever felt like that? Or have you ever glimpsed a shooting star? Whoosh—and it's gone. Did it really happen?

Jesus had done something amazing, feeding all those people. But now he'd sent them all away. He'd even gone away himself, and the disciples were out fishing in the middle of the night. Had it really happened—or had they imagined it?

Jesus knew how they felt. So he came to them, walking on the water, to show that nothing is impossible for him to do.

People in a hurry
Mark 6:53–56

So they ran throughout the whole region; and wherever they heard he was, they brought to him sick people lying on their mats. (Verse 55)

What do you like doing best on a very hot day? Maybe splashing about in a swimming-pool or the sea. Maybe sitting under a shady tree with a cool can of Coke. Or maybe doing something entirely different. It's nice even to think about it. The last thing you want is to go running about the country-side carrying heavy weights.

Mark, full of energy and enthusiasm, must have loved this story. The place where Jesus lived was very hot indeed. But to the people of Gennesaret the visit of Jesus was very important. They were prepared to go tearing around telling their friends and carrying sick people to him. And he made them well!

How important is Jesus to us? Are we prepared to make extra efforts to bring people to him?

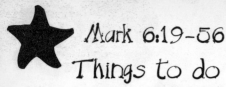

Mark 6:19-56
Things to do

How many?

You'll need to get your friends to help you with this. Each take a piece of A4 paper and a thick crayon or marker pen and mark out ten blobs in a row along the top, then mark out twenty-five in a row down the side. Now carefully put in all the in-between blobs, going across the rows. You'll need to fill in twenty sheets altogether. Lay the pages out side by side, or put them all up on the wall, and see just how many people Jesus fed!

Toby + Trish   How many?

How many eggs does a peacock lay in its lifetime?

Must be a lot, I suppose

No, none, silly! The peahen lays the eggs!

We've always done it this way
Mark 7:1–8

So the Pharisees and the teachers of the Law asked Jesus, 'Why is it that your disciples do not follow the teaching handed down by our ancestors?' (Verse 5)

There was once an old lady who carefully cut her bacon into 10 cm lengths before she fried it—so she usually had shrivelled-up bits of bacon to eat! One day a visitor asked her why she did this. 'When I was a little girl,' said the old lady, 'my mother always did that because she had a very tiny frying pan.' 'But you have a very big frying pan,' said the visitor. 'You could fry beautiful whole rashers of bacon.' 'No, I couldn't,' said the old lady, 'I've always done it this way.'

You hear people saying that so often—in shops, in churches, schools… anywhere. They are following rules that once were probably necessary, but now sometimes have no meaning at all.

If we follow Jesus, everything we do will make sense—because he's concerned with today… not yesterday!

41

It's what's inside that counts
Mark 7:14-15

'Rather, it is what comes out of a person that makes him unclean.' (Verse 15)

Have you ever chosen the best-looking apple in the dish—it's red and shiny and looks perfect—and taken a great big bite? Ugh! It tastes horrid. Under the skin it's brown and nasty and at the centre is an awful little brown grub. You can't always tell from the outside what apples are like... or people either.

It's easy for us to be all show—saying the right things, being in the right place, wearing the right clothes, doing things a certain way.

But what really counts is *why* we are saying, and being, and doing. We can't pretend with Jesus. He knows what we're like, in our hearts, where it really matters.

Dear Jesus, be in my heart so that everything I do and say will please you. Amen

I thought this would interest Boomerang!

Crumbs of faith
Mark 7:24–30

'Sir,' she answered, 'even the dogs under the table eat the children's leftovers!' (Verse 28)

The woman must have been very brave and very determined. But she was desperate. Although she'd been born in Syria, she actually asked a Jewish teacher for an enormous favour! The Jews and the Syrians had been enemies for a long time. (Those old rules again!) They never mixed.

Because she was not a Jew, the woman should have expected nothing from Jesus—but she asked anyway. And he tested her by telling a little parable. She was prepared to stand right at the 'back of the queue'—anything, anything, if only he would make her daughter better.

Because of her great love for her daughter and her great faith in him, Jesus then did an amazing thing. He healed the girl without even seeing her. Love is stronger than rules.

To hear and to speak
Mark 7:31–37

Then Jesus looked up to heaven, gave a deep groan, and said to the man, 'Ephphatha,' which means, 'Open up!' (Verse 34)

If you play a wind instrument, maybe a recorder or a clarinet, or if you've watched somebody else playing one, you'll know how they work. You blow in at one end and, by using your fingers to control the air inside, a lovely tune comes out at the other end. You hope!

But what happens if the instrument gets blocked up? You can blow until you're blue in the face and you get either a strange noise from the other end... or nothing at all.

The man's ears were blocked and, because he couldn't hear others speaking, his own speech sounded strange. Jesus cared deeply about him and showed it by the special way in which he made him well.

Lord Jesus, open our ears to hear your voice so that we may speak the right words about you to other people. Amen

I'm thinking again...

They would not see
Mark 8:11-13

But Jesus gave a deep groan and said, 'Why do the people of this age ask for a miracle? No, I tell you! No such proof will be given to these people!' (Verse 12)

Have you ever played 'Hunt the Thimble'? It's great fun! You look under the settee or in the teapot because you expect it to be somewhere like that—but it's not there. Then suddenly you find it, right under your nose, in the place you've walked past several times.

The Pharisees were looking for God in their temple and in their laws, because that's where they expected to find him. They couldn't see God himself, Jesus, standing under their very noses. Neither *would* they see and understand the wonderful things that he was doing.

Jesus realized that whatever he did the Pharisees would never be convinced he was God. Their own strict ideas stopped them from recognizing him.

Dear Jesus, if my own ideas are stopping me from knowing you better, help me to think again. Amen

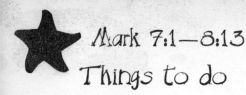

Mark 7:1—8:13

Things to do

Open up!

Put your fingers in your ears and listen. You won't hear nothing—you'll hear your heartbeat and your breathing. Now speak out aloud. You'll hear the sound of your own voice, but you won't hear anybody else, so you won't be able to hold a conversation with them. And you won't know how loudly or softly you are speaking. Now take your fingers out of your ears and listen carefully. Count the number of different sounds that come rushing in. Imagine that the voice of Jesus is one of them!

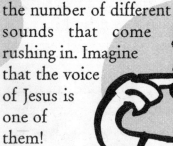

Toby + Trish — Listen up!

I'm going to start selling this...

WHAT IS IT?

Silence!

Not just about bread
Mark 8:14-19

Jesus knew what they were saying, so he asked them, 'Why are you discussing about not having any bread? Don't you know or understand yet? Are your minds so dull?' (Verse 17)

Once there was a woman who told an awful lie. Then, feeling bad about it, she went to see the priest. He handed her a bag of goose feathers, and said, 'Walk through the forest scattering them as you go. Then come back.' Surprised, she did so. 'Now,' said the priest, 'go and gather up the feathers.' 'That's impossible,' said the lady. 'Exactly. Likewise, once you have lied, or been unkind, the results can never be undone. They spread, like the feathers blowing through the forest.'

In the same way, Jesus describes our faults as being like yeast that spreads—food containing yeast can eventually go nasty.

The disciples were good men—*their* main fault was that they were slow to understand Jesus' teaching. To them a loaf was just something to eat. But Jesus was patient with them—just as he is with us.

Seeing things as they really are
Mark 8:22-26

*The man looked up and said, 'Yes,
I can see people, but they look like
trees walking about.' (Verse 24)*

Sometimes if you're out when it's just getting dark, you see a shape in the distance. Particularly if you're in a strange place, you don't know what it is, and you imagine it's all sorts of odd things. Then, as you get closer, it stops being just a shape. It becomes a bush...

This story is similar to the one about the deaf man who couldn't speak properly. They're so alive with detail and are only found in Mark's gospel. Peter must have been there as our special reporter!

There's one difference—this man wasn't healed immediately. At first he saw people who looked like trees!

Sometimes we don't see or understand things clearly at first, like the blind man—and the disciples in the previous reading. But as we get closer to Jesus we will see things as they really are.

Who do you think I am?
Mark 8:27-30

'What about you?' he asked them. 'Who do you say I am?' (Verse 29)

If you listen to gossip about somebody, maybe at school, it's difficult to know what *you* think about them. The best thing is to get to know the person better and make up your own mind.

By now Jesus was the talk of the district. Everybody was gossiping about him... so many points of view... who was he? Think of some of the people Jesus had met and imagine what they would say.

There was only one right answer. And it was given by somebody who knew Jesus better than anybody else—Peter. At last Peter called Jesus the Messiah—the one promised by God from the very beginning. At last he and the disciples were beginning to understand who Jesus was.

Lord Jesus, help me to understand who you really are. Amen

48

God's hard way for Jesus
Mark 8:31-33

Then Jesus began to teach his disciples: 'The Son of Man must suffer much and be rejected by the elders, the chief priests and the teachers of the Law. He will be put to death, but three days later he will rise to life.' (Verse 31)

It's not easy learning to ride a bicycle. The wheels seem too thin and it's a nasty moment when you first take both feet off the ground and set off. You wobble all over the place until finally you think you've got it sorted... then you hit a bump, lose your balance and come a cropper!

The disciples had come a cropper, just when *they* thought they'd got it sorted. They'd thought the Messiah would free them from the rule of the Romans. Jesus was the Messiah... *yes.* But he was a different sort of Messiah. He would suffer in every way to free them from something far worse than the Romans—the power of evil.

The disciples wanted Jesus to do it their way. They still had lots to learn about Jesus' own way.

Lord Jesus, help me to learn that your way is best. Amen

10 seconds and counting

Blast off
with Jesus
Mark 8:34-38

*Then Jesus called the crowds and his
disciples to him. 'If anyone wants to come with
me,' he told them, 'he must forget self,
carry his cross, and follow me.' (Verse 34)*

Let's pretend we're off on a space mission. We
know lots about it from films and books. First...
the months of preparation, which will be fun—and
hard work. Then... *blast off!* There's no turning
back now. It won't be easy. It might be dangerous.
But oh, the excitement! There we are, looking down
on the world—and much more!

The disciples must have enjoyed travelling round
Galilee with Jesus. Sunny days, listening and
watching, long walks! But now they're coming to
the nitty-gritty—it's almost time for blast off.
There's no turning back. It won't be easy. There'll
be difficult decisions to make. Following Jesus has to
be more important than anything else. But oh, the
excitement. And the surprises.

If we follow Jesus he will make a world of difference to us—and much more!

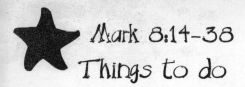

Mark 8:14-38

Things to do

Following Jesus

JOY

JESUS FIRST

OTHERS IN BETWEEN

YOURSELF LAST

Using a cereal packet or some card, cut out the three letters, J O Y, as big as you can. Now write 'Jesus first' on the 'J', 'Others in between' on the 'O' and 'Yourself last' on the 'Y'. Display the letters where you'll be able to see them every day to remind yourself what it means to follow Jesus.

Toby + Trish — Easy to follow?

I love line dancing –'s easy

Yes, you just follow the person in front...

...until you all turn round, then they follow you!

Ouch! Bump! Wallop!

I'd like to be a king—you'd get everything king-size!

The other side of Jesus
Mark 9:2-13

As they looked on, a change came over Jesus, and his clothes became shining white—whiter than anyone in the world could wash them. (Verses 2–3)

There's an elderly man in our village who, like all elderly men, was once a little boy. He tells the story of how one day the people from the 'big house' and a bearded man walked past where he was playing. The bearded man came over to him and they talked and laughed together.

Afterwards the boy's mother said, 'You must feel very proud talking to the king like that.' 'He couldn't have been the king,' said the little boy. 'He wasn't wearing a crown.' A few days later, in the newspaper was a picture of King George V—wearing his crown. 'It was the king,' said the little boy.

Although Jesus had said and done amazing things, the disciples still thought of him as just a man. Now they needed to see him in a different light—as God.

Jesus, the friend who understands us, is also the king of the whole world.

Everything is possible
Mark 9:14-24

'Yes,' said Jesus, 'if you yourself can! Everything is possible for the person who has faith.' (Verse 23)

Gladys Aylward was a small woman with a big faith. She was a missionary in China and one day they said to her, 'There's a riot in the prison. They're killing each other. We daren't go inside. But you've said that your God can do anything—go and stop it.' Gladys was terrified—but she prayed, then she went inside and shouted above the noise. And the riot stopped.

The disciples had special things to do for Jesus. 'Everything is possible.' But they didn't yet have enough faith to 'flick the switch' and let God's power work through them as it did through Jesus.

We too have our own things to do for Jesus. First, we need to find out what they are. Then we need to flick that switch of faith so that his power will come through and help us to do them. 'Everything is possible.'

The last journey begins
Mark 9:30-32

But they did not understand what this teaching meant, and they were afraid to ask him. (Verse 32)

When an ostrich thinks that something terrible is going to happen he hides his head in the sand. He thinks that because he can't see anything, nothing can see him and the trouble will go away. (He forgets about his big feathery bottom sticking up in the air!)

The disciples were setting out with Jesus on his last journey to Jerusalem. They loved Jesus and couldn't—wouldn't—understand the terrible things he was telling them would happen. They thought that if they didn't ask questions, and hid from the truth, the trouble would go away.

Not so. Travelling with Jesus means learning to face up to things, however unpleasant. That way, with his help, we will also learn not to be afraid.

Lord God, help us to face up to unpleasant things—and win through in the end. Amen

Who is the greatest?
Mark 9:33-37

Jesus sat down, called the twelve disciples, and said to them, 'Whoever wants to be first must place himself last of all and be the servant of all.' (Verse 35)

There was once a spider who dropped, on a single strand, from a dark corner into the light. 'What a good place to spin a web,' he thought. So he set to work. Soon the silken threads spread in all directions. It was a beautiful web. The spider felt very proud of himself. 'Now I don't need the strong strand I dropped down on,' he said. So he cut it. And because that strong strand was holding up the web, everything, including the spider, fell to the floor and became just dust.

Being the most important is not important. We become proud of ourselves and think we can manage on our own without the person we need most—Jesus.

If we forget about ourselves and think about other people instead, we will be important to Jesus. And that's what really matters.

Maps are great but I can't fold them up

54

We're all different
Mark 9:38-40

John said to him, 'Teacher, we saw a man who was driving out demons in your name, and we told him to stop, because he doesn't belong to our group.' (Verse 38)

Maps are fascinating, particularly those that cover part of the country on a big scale. Have a look at one. Then choose a place and notice how many roads lead to it. Different kinds of roads... some may be fast motorways, others quiet country lanes, but they all finish up at the same place.

We're all different from each other. The world would be a very boring place if we weren't! And there are many different ways leading to Jesus. Different churches with different sorts of services, different ways of showing our love for him. Your way may be the best for you—it may not be the best for somebody else.

And however different we may be, Jesus will always be the same.

 Thank you, Jesus, for our 'differentness'. Help us to learn from each other. Amen

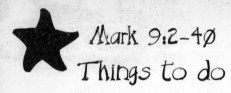

Mark 9:2-40
Things to do

Seeing Jesus in a new light

For centuries people have been trying to show Jesus shining in stained-glass windows. See if you can make one, too. Cut a window shape out of the side of a cereal packet and stick a piece of grease-proof paper over the hole. Use a thick black marker pen to draw a picture of Jesus. Use felt-tipped pens to colour in his face, hands and feet and the background. Leave his clothes white. Now hold your window in front of a lamp or against strong sunlight and see if you are dazzled like Peter, James and John.

Toby + Trish — Stained all right

My teacher said I'm like a stained-glass window!

HUH!

Well, she said I'm colourful and quite bright

Sometimes in shops I see myself on closed-circuit television

Watch it!
Mark 9:42-47

'If anyone should cause one of these little ones to lose his faith in me, it would be better for that person to have a large millstone tied round his neck and be thrown into the sea.' (Verse 42)

Every day Jesus and the disciples came nearer to Jerusalem. It was absolutely essential for the disciples to realize just what being a disciple meant. Jesus is speaking in parables here—it has nothing to do with doctors and operations. He is trying to shock them into some serious thinking.

Yesterday they were told to be gentle and understanding with other people. Today they are told to be hard on themselves.

'Watch it,' Jesus is saying. 'Anything in you—greed, envy, untruthfulness—that shouldn't be there, get rid of it. People are watching you because you are my friends. If *you* behave badly they may decide they don't want to know *me*.

And so it is with us. 'Watch it.' People are watching *us*. Are we a good advertisement for Jesus?

Dear Lord, help us not to get in the way of anybody else wanting to know you. Amen

Love can last
Mark 10:1-9

'...and the two will become one. So they are no longer two, but one.' (Verse 8)

'And they lived happily ever after.' Phew! After all the adventures and close shaves, this is how every good fairy-tale ends. But what about real life?

We're a mixture of feelings, some good, some bad... greed, hate, love. Think of some more. And how we deal with these feelings affects how we get on with other people.

The strongest feeling of all is love. It weakens the bad feelings; it doesn't go away when problems come; it forgives... and forgives. If we love someone, our selfishness grows weak—we think more about that person than we think about ourselves.

When two people marry, they promise God to love each other always—no matter what happens. And God, who knows all about love, will help them keep that promise... if they really want him to.

Yes, they *will* live happily ever after.

Fish and chips—
You can hear them,
see them, touch
them, taste them,
smell them

God's children
Mark 10:13-16

*'I assure you that whoever does
not receive the Kingdom of God like
a child will never enter it.' (Verse 15)*

On holiday I watched a very small boy sitting by the edge of the sea. He was holding a pebble in his hand, smooth and warm from the sun. He stared at its whiteness, then sniffed its salty sea smell. And then, wanting to taste it, he opened his mouth to pop it in. 'Not in your mouth,' said his mother. So he threw it into the sea... plop! All of himself, all five senses, had been fascinated by his wonderful pebble. Luckily, he heard his mother's voice and she knew what was best for him.

As we get older, if we're not careful, we don't notice God's wonderful gifts to us. We're too busy, and worried, and think we can manage on our own. And we don't hear Jesus telling us what is best for us.

Dear Jesus, help us always to know the wonder of what you have given us. Amen

58

Too much to pay
Mark 10:17-22

Jesus looked straight at him with love and said, 'You need only one thing. Go and sell all you have and give your money to the poor, and you will have riches in heaven; then come and follow me.' (Verse 21)

It isn't that Jesus is against money—we all need it to get by on, and he knows that. But when it becomes the most important thing in our lives... that's when we might be heading for trouble.

But it's not only money that can 'take us over'. Maybe we'd do *anything* to be popular, or to be thinner, or fatter, or own that bicycle we've seen in a shop window in town. Maybe we can't think about anything else but that.

The man was a good man, he did all the right things, and he knew Jesus was special. But still his money and his possessions meant more to him than following Jesus.

Jesus loves us, and he wants us to enjoy life. But if we had to choose, would we put him first, before anything else?

A bit of a squash
Mark 10:23-27

'It is much harder for a rich man to enter the Kingdom of God than for a camel to go through the eye of a needle.' (Verse 25)

Jesus liked a joke. Just imagine a camel going through the eye of a needle, hump and all! Ouch! The more important the place, the harder it is to get in.

Castles are important—and exciting. Usually they're very old and although nowadays they're easy to get into, they weren't always.

They were surrounded by a moat that could only be crossed by a drawbridge that was let up and down. Then there was the portcullis, a huge door of metal bars that only opened from the inside. Knights in full armour on horseback, and carts, passed through here. Then... look carefully. In the portcullis is a tiny door, just wide enough to let you and me walk in, carrying nothing.

In the end all our belongings are just clutter. Jesus wants us just as we are. He loves us just as we are.

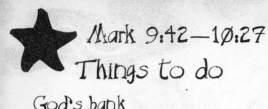

Mark 9:42—10:27

Things to do

God's bank

The rich man had lots of money, but not much in the bank of heaven. Make your own cheque book and bank card for God's bank. In the cheque book, write something kind and helpful you could do for someone else. You can use the bank card to draw on God's love any time you like!

GOD'S BANK — Date ——— signed
For ——
I will ——

GOD'S BANK
God's love is available
24 hours a day
VALID FROM NOW
TO ETERNITY

Toby + Trish   God's bank

Did you know, Trish, you can get rich by folding up a £5 note and sitting on it?

You'll find your money in creases

Jumping the queue
Mark 10:28-31

'But many who now are first will be last, and many who now are last will be first.' (Verse 31)

We're used to standing in orderly queues—at supermarkets, the bank, the bus stop. But in some countries it's different.

The bus arrives and there's a mad scramble towards the door at the front. The strong ones push and shove and the gentle ones find themselves at the back. When the door opens they get on last. But just a few buses have *two* doors. Imagine what happens if the *back* door opens as well. Ahh! Yes!

'Just look at us. We've given up everything to follow you. We're at the front,' says Peter. But following Jesus doesn't mean boasting about what we've done, or what we haven't got. That way we might miss the wonderful blessings that Jesus wants to give us. We might miss the bus altogether.

A sad journey
Mark 10:32-34

Jesus and his disciples were now on the road going up to Jerusalem. Jesus was going ahead of the disciples, who were filled with alarm; the people who followed behind were afraid. Once again Jesus took the twelve disciples aside and spoke of the things that were going to happen to him. (Verse 32)

Have you ever been out walking when there's a thunderstorm brewing? The sky is dark and feels heavy, on top of you. There's a stillness—even the birds have stopped singing, as though everything's waiting for something to happen. The 'hugeness' of it all makes you feel uneasy, alarmed, because you know you can't do anything to stop it when it does happen.

The disciples were feeling like that. Jesus was striding ahead towards the terrible events that hung like a cloud over them, that they didn't understand and couldn't do anything to stop.

And Jesus put aside his own feelings to explain it to them once more. He wanted them to understand—just as he wants us to understand.

Help us, Lord Jesus, to understand why you had to go to Jerusalem. Amen

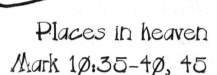

Anybody eating
my porridge—you're
welcome to it!

Places in heaven
Mark 10:35-40, 45

'I do not have the right to choose who will sit at my right and my left. It is God who will give these places to those for whom he has prepared them.' (Verse 40)

'Who's been sitting in my chair?' said each of the three bears. We all get a bit put out if we find a stranger is sitting in our place—on the school bus, at school dinners... even in church. 'Newcomers are OK as long as they don't get in my way,' is what we're saying.

At least James and John understood that there *was* a kingdom of God. Jesus must have been pleased about that. But they were aiming for the best for themselves—a seat next to Jesus at the 'top table'.

These arrangements are in God's hands—even Jesus was ready to give up his place and become a servant when God wanted him to.

Jesus, help me to be ready to do things for others, even when I don't want to. Amen

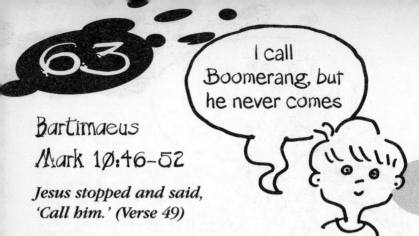

I call Boomerang, but he never comes

Bartimaeus
Mark 10:46-52

Jesus stopped and said, 'Call him.' (Verse 49)

People were used to Bartimaeus calling out. After all, he was a beggar and a bit of a nuisance. But when he started calling out to Jesus, well... they were embarrassed. 'Shut up,' they told him.

But Bartimaeus wouldn't shut up. He was pleading for far more than money—and he was desperate. Somehow he knew that Jesus was special—chosen by God—and could help him. This could be his last chance ever to be able to see.

The footsteps got nearer, deafening noises, loud voices. What chance had he of being heard? Were they going to pass him by?

No! The footsteps stopped. Everything went quiet. Then, 'Call him.' Jesus had heard Bartimaeus not with his ears but with his heart.

Just as he hears everyone who is desperate and frightened that he will pass them by.

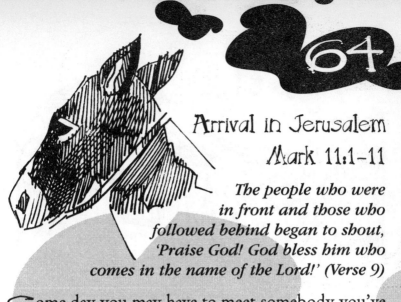

Arrival in Jerusalem
Mark 11:1-11

*The people who were
in front and those who
followed behind began to shout,
'Praise God! God bless him who
comes in the name of the Lord!' (Verse 9)*

Some day you may have to meet somebody you've never seen before. How will you know it's them? You choose a particular place—under a station clock maybe—and you ask them to wear or carry something you'll recognize them by. At airports people hold up cards with their names on, so that the person meeting them will know who they are.

It was time for Jesus to show clearly who he was. So he chose his place, Jerusalem, and his transport, a donkey, and he did what the Jewish scriptures said God's chosen one would do. The donkey—a symbol of a king coming in peace—he had to borrow!

He knew he was riding into trouble, but this was all part of God's plan for him.

*Help us, dear God, to show who
we are—followers of Jesus. Amen*

Things to do

Hooray for Jesus!

They didn't have a red carpet in those days, so they made a carpet with their cloaks and branches from the palm trees that lined the road. This was the carpet the donkey walked on to show that Jesus was a VIP.

Write what it said in the newspaper next day—what people thought about Jesus, where he had come from, what he had done, and what his future plans were.

Toby + Trish

Why do they print a newspaper every day...

...even when there isn't any news?

I once cracked a nut and it was empty

No use to anybody
Mark 11:12-14

Jesus saw in the distance a fig tree covered with leaves, so he went to see if he could find any figs on it. But when he came to it, he found only leaves, because it was not the right time for figs. (Verse 13)

Just imagine it's your birthday, or Christmas, and somebody has given you a wonderful present. At least, it looks good from the outside. Brightly coloured paper tied up with that tape that you can make into curly tassels at the end. You get that off and underneath is a beautiful patterned box. But when you whip the lid off there's nothing inside. What use is a box that's empty, even if it does look good from the outside?

The fig tree looked good. Nice leaves—but you can't eat leaves. No fruit—no use!

The religion of the Jewish people looked good. But the way some people behaved was *not* good. They were like nicely wrapped-up empty boxes, or fruitless fig trees. They had no thoughtfulness, no love, no 'fruit'. They were no use to anybody.

Boomerang only barks at us, so he's no guard dog

Turning the tables
Mark 11:15-19

Jesus then taught the people: 'It is written in the Scriptures that God said, "My Temple will be called a house of prayer for the people of all nations." But you have turned it into a hideout for thieves!' (Verse 17)

Your house, where you live with your family, is a special place to you. It's therefore very upsetting if something awful happens in that house. People who have been burgled say that the worst thing is not money and valuables being stolen—although that's bad enough! It's that thieves have been looking through all their things, searching drawers and cupboards, touching furniture. Everything feels dirty.

Jesus felt like that, only much worse, when he went into the temple. This was supposed to be his Father's house of prayer. The thieves—those people who were exchanging money and selling things dishonestly—were still there. Everything felt dirty. No wonder he couldn't help but turn them all out.

Anger is sometimes necessary if it makes things clean again.

The power of prayer
Mark 11:20-26

Jesus answered them,
'Have faith in God.' (Verse 22)

Near where I live there's a place called 'Buffers'. It's a farm and little café and in the loft above the café are wonderful electric train layouts. Tunnels, bridges, villages, factories, trees, animals, people and, of course, trains, lines and stations. Carefully planned and made by 'Mr Buffers', you can set everything going and the little lights twinkling just by pressing a button.

Prayer is like that. God made us and has a plan for each of us, but we need to start everything moving by 'pressing the button' of prayer. There is no limit to what God can do for us through prayer—but we need to really believe this.

If we follow Jesus he will teach us what to pray for. Then God's plan for us will really come to life.

What can go up a drainpipe down, but can't go down a drainpipe up?

A riddle
Mark 11:27–33

Jesus answered them, 'I will ask you just one question, and if you give me an answer, I will tell you what right I have to do these things. Tell me, where did John's right to baptize come from: was it from God or from human beings?' (Verses 29–30)

Question: What is yellow and white and travels at a hundred miles an hour? Answer: A train driver's egg sandwich.

We all like riddles, and usually the answers are either very silly or very difficult.

The question the chief priests and elders asked Jesus was like a riddle, but they weren't just having fun. He had said and done lots of things they didn't like and they were trying to trap him into saying something he could be arrested for.

Jesus knew this, but he was cleverer than they were. He asked *them* a question in return. Whichever way they answered it they would displease somebody —and they didn't want to do that. So they said they didn't know the answer and slunk away.

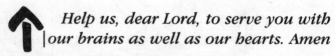

Help us, dear Lord, to serve you with our brains as well as our hearts. Amen

Murder in the vineyard
Mark 12:1-8

But those tenants said to one another, 'This is the owner's son. Come on, let's kill him, and his property will be ours!' (Verse 7)

Some of the things we've got belong to us; others are just on loan—a library book, a musical instrument—can you think of others? On holiday we rent rooms, or houses, cars, boats... they're not ours, but we must look after them as if they were.

We're living in God's world, and he expects us to look after it carefully, as if it were ours. But do we? Even if we don't personally cut down too many trees, put nasty things in the rivers and seas, or spoil the fresh air with poisons, there are plenty of things we *do* do that spoil his world.

Jesus is telling a parable. The vineyard is God's world. Down the ages people have tried hard to pretend this isn't true. And still do so!

Lord of all, help me to live in your world in a loving, caring way. Amen

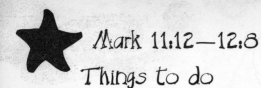

Mark 11:12—12:8

Things to do

Getting angry

If something isn't right—like robbing people in the temple—there is nothing wrong with getting angry about it. Jesus did. Think of something that is wrong in our world—something you have seen on TV like landmines, drugs, killing wildlife, or stealing food from starving people—and make a poster in which you show your anger and explain why we must try to stop it.

DRUGS HURT PEOPLE HELP TO STOP THEM

Toby + Trish

Mum gets angry

Why is it that when Boomerang makes muddy paw marks on the floor, Mum gets mad with me...

...but when I make muddy marks, she doesn't get mad with Boomerang?

Football rules
are simple:
we lose

What belongs to whom?
Mark 12:13-17

*So Jesus said, 'Well, then, pay the
Emperor **what belongs to the Emperor,
and pay God what belongs to God.'**
And they were amazed at Jesus. (Verse 17)*

Imagine someone saying, 'Right! No more rules or
laws. Do exactly as you like.' You'd have a ball—
until you realized the same had been said to everybody else. Chaos on the roads, empty supermarket
shelves, no meals ready, no TV, because people
didn't feel like working. Not so good.

We need rules because our lives need a pattern,
and although we grumble, we need to respect those
rules and the people who make them. Grown-ups
need to pay taxes because fixing rules and governing
a country costs money.

It's those Pharisees again, trying to catch Jesus
out. Does his loyalty lie with the Roman conquerors,
or with God? But Jesus shows that it's possible—
and necessary—to be loyal to those in authority *and*
to God. Both at the same time.

*Lord God, help me to respect those
whom you have put in authority. Amen*

Making God too small
Mark 12:18–27

'He is the God of the living, not of the dead. You are completely wrong!' (Verse 27)

There are lots of books and films about time warps, where people suddenly travel backwards, or forwards, hundred of years. It could be fun. God deals in hundreds of millions of years—yet in some ways, time to God is always 'today'. It's hard for us to imagine.

Even harder, what is heaven like? It will be full of life, full of feelings, not just as we know them, but as God knows them... like taking off your sunglasses and earplugs in a lovely garden and really seeing and understanding.

We try to tie God down to the way *we* do things. But Jesus came to show us how *God* does things— to show us that real life can start now and last for ever.

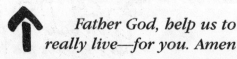

Father God, help us to really live—for you. Amen

The greatest commandment
Mark 12:28-34

*'Love the Lord your God with all your
heart, with all your soul, with all your mind,
and with all your strength.' (Verse 30)*

Have you ever seen how a cartoonist draws? He does lots of lines all over the place, then suddenly, with the last one, the whole thing comes together and makes sense. It is complete.

It's little use loving God with just part of us. We may be willing to go to church every Sunday, but when we get there we daydream about something else. We may say we'll do that old lady's shopping, but somehow we go swimming instead.

But if we really love God with every single bit of us, then Jesus will be that final line that brings us together and makes us complete.

73

Boomerang visits his family tree every day

More than just 'Son of David'
Mark 12:35-37

'David himself called him "Lord"; so how can the Messiah be David's descendant?' (Verse 37)

Some people like trying to trace their 'family tree'. They hunt through old papers, and even church-yards, until they discover who their great-great-grandfather was. And even further back than that! Maybe your family sailed from France with William the Conqueror in 1066!

People who know the Bible very well have traced Jesus' family tree—right back to King David, who wrote some of the lovely Psalms. But although Jesus is sometimes called 'Son of David' he is much more than that. Even mighty King David called God's Messiah 'Lord', showing that when he came the Messiah would be king of kings.

Jesus has come. God's chosen Messiah, king of kings and lord of lords, has come.

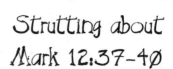

Strutting about
Mark 12:37-40

*As he taught them, he said,
'Watch out for the teachers of
the Law, who like to walk around
in their long robes and be greeted
with respect in the market place.' (Verse 38)*

There's a rather naughty story about an emperor who was very vain—he liked new clothes and he thought he was very clever. One day his tailor said, 'Sire, I have here some material so finely woven that only the cleverest can see it.' Now, the emperor could see nothing, but because he wanted to be thought the cleverest, he wouldn't say so. So he ordered a suit to be made from it.

When the suit arrived he still couldn't see anything, but he put it on and strutted before his courtiers. They couldn't see the suit either—but they didn't dare say so. The crafty tailor had played a trick—there was really nothing there—the emperor was walking about absolutely... well...!

Jesus is not taken in by what we wear, or by what we think of ourselves. He can see through all that—to the real person underneath.

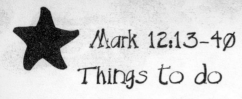

Mark 12:13-40

Things to do

Four-way love

Using a piece of card, make a mobile with a large card at the top and four smaller cards hanging underneath. On the large card write the words 'Love God' and on the smaller cards show the four different kinds of love that Jesus talks about in Mark 12:30.

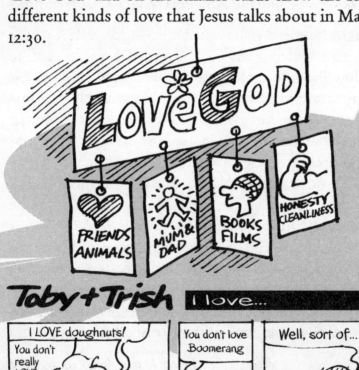

Toby + Trish — I love...

I LOVE doughnuts!

You don't really LOVE them

Not like I love animals, like rabbits and dolphins

You don't love Boomerang

Well, sort of...

It's what's left that matters
Mark 12:41-44

'For the others put in what they had to spare of their riches; but she, poor as she is, put in all she had—she gave all she had to live on.' (Verse 44)

Eight hundred years ago there lived in Italy a young man called Francesco. One day he decided to follow Jesus and, although he was very rich, he gave away everything he had. The rest of his life was spent caring for the poor and the ill; even the animals loved him. We know him today as St Francis of Assisi.

The poor widow also gave everything she had— one penny.

The gift of this widow and the gift of St Francis were the same to God. Because it's not what we give that's important… it's what's left afterwards that matters. What have we kept back for ourselves?

Not just money either. Jesus wants our time, our thoughts, our ideas—and most of all our love.

 Dear Jesus, help us to give everything we are to you Amen.

When everything topples
Mark 13:1-4

Jesus answered, 'You see these great buildings? Not a single stone here will be left in its place; every one of them will be thrown down.' (Verse 2)

In April 1912 a beautiful ship sailed from England on her first voyage, heading towards America. She was the *Titanic*, the biggest liner in the world. 'She's absolutely unsinkable,' her builders said with pride and joy. But before she reached America she hit an iceberg—and sank. Hundreds of people were drowned. Where was the pride and joy then?

The Jewish people thought that the temple in Jerusalem was like that. It was beautiful, it would last for ever, it was their pride and joy.

But Jesus warned against having faith in things made by human hands. Before long their beautiful temple would topple.

Sometimes things we have known and trusted seem to fall apart around us, too.

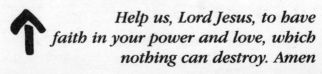

Help us, Lord Jesus, to have faith in your power and love, which nothing can destroy. Amen

Hold on
Mark 13:5-10, 13

'Everyone will hate you because of me. But whoever holds out to the end will be saved.' (Verse 13)

When you throw a pebble into a pond the ripples spread to all sides until they reach the edge.

In a way, Jesus is like that pebble. He had come to take on all the forces of wickedness in the world, starting in a small corner called Galilee. His own suffering was nearly on him. And from that suffering the ripples would spread... and spread. It almost seemed that because Jesus was absolute goodness, the power of absolute wickedness was being released, like some dreadful wild animal from a cage.

The disciples too would suffer. Things would happen around them that they couldn't begin to understand.

'But hold on,' says Jesus. 'Don't give in. In the end my strength will save you.'

We don't know what the future holds...

The last battle
Mark 13:14-23

*'Be on your guard!
I have told you
everything before the time comes.' (Verse 23)*

Nothing comes as a surprise to God. And here is Jesus giving plenty of warning of troubles ahead because he is God and knows what's in the future.

We sometimes say, 'It's not fair'—and sometimes it isn't. Things can be topsy-turvy and confusing. Dishonest and wicked people seem to get away with things and gentle people suffer. 'It's not fair.' But evil won't just go away on its own—it has to be fought and defeated.

It isn't easy. But if you read Psalm 46, maybe with a grown-up, there is God's promise that he will be with us no matter what happens.

And when the ripple finally reaches the edge, and the last battle is won...

...but we know who holds the future

Jesus will come again
Mark 13:24-27

'Then the Son of Man will appear, coming in the clouds with great power and glory.' (Verse 26)

Jesus *will* come again.

After everything seems to have fallen apart, and even the stars seem to have lost their way... Jesus *will* come again.

In a way, Jesus' promise is like the wonderful story of creation backwards. What God created was beautiful, but people have made it ugly and there's a lot of wickedness about. All this must go, until it will be like the beginning again when God said, 'Let there be light.' Jesus is our light, and he *will* come again.

This time there will be no mistaking who he is—no manger, no stable—he is the king of kings and everybody will know it. 'It isn't fair' will never, ever, be heard again—because everything will be... very fair.

The word 'fair' has another meaning—it can also mean 'beautiful'.

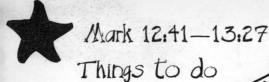

Mark 12:41—13:27

Things to do

Night and day

Cut a piece of A4 paper in half and on one half use dark colours to draw a picture showing houses falling down and people running away. On the other half use light colours of white and gold to draw a picture of Jesus coming in clouds of glory. Now carefully cut each picture into vertical strips, 1 cm in width. Stick the pictures to an A4 sheet of paper in the right order, but alternating the dark and light strips. Fan-fold the finished picture so that all the dark strips look left and all the light strips look right. Tape the fan-folded picture to a piece of stiff card. Then, by moving the card from side to side, you will see both pictures at once. There's no need to worry—Jesus is coming!

Toby + Trish — Night and day

Why do cats sleep all day and go out at night?

While dogs sleep all day and all night as well!

SNORE

My favourite word is 'always'.

One thing is certain
Mark 13:28-31

'Heaven and earth will pass away, but my words will never pass away.' (Verse 31)

A friend is not a friend unless you can trust what they say. It's no good their saying, 'I'll come round in the morning' if you wait and wait but they never come. Or you're sad and they say, 'If there's anything I can do, let me know', then they go off with somebody else. Words are important— written down or spoken—and they have to mean something.

Jesus is a friend we can trust. There are a lot of things we thought we could rely on that maybe won't be so sure. But we *can* rely on the words of Jesus.

At the start of John's gospel we read, 'In the beginning the Word already existed'—God's promise. Jesus says, 'My words will never pass away'—Jesus' promise. In the beginning, and for ever, we can trust Jesus and what he says.

Dear Jesus, help me to really mean what I say to other people, or not to say it at all. Amen

I can tie my shoelaces—but not when you're watching

Keep watch!
Mark 13:32-37

'Be on watch, be alert, for you do not know when the time will come.' (Verse 33)

If you run a restaurant (you may, some day) it can be a worry. Because now and then a person comes in, sits at a table and orders a meal—and then goes away and writes about it. So everybody will know if you serve lumpy custard, or meat-and-potato pie with no meat. The trouble is, you're given no warning. If you knew beforehand, you'd make sure your custard was smooth and your pie meaty.

When Jesus comes a second time, there'll be no warning. It's no good saying, 'I'll do as I like now, then pull my socks up when he comes', because you'll be caught out.

It's better to remember that even now he is with us. That way you'll be ready to receive him in all his power and glory.

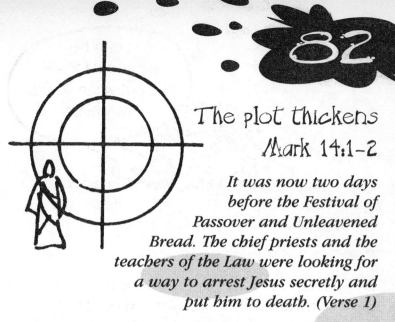

The plot thickens
Mark 14:1-2

It was now two days before the Festival of Passover and Unleavened Bread. The chief priests and the teachers of the Law were looking for a way to arrest Jesus secretly and put him to death. (Verse 1)

Jerusalem was like a firework waiting to explode. It was packed with excited people who had come for the festival; on top of that, Jesus had chosen this time to enter the city as the Messiah and everybody seemed overjoyed about it.

The chief priests and teachers had had enough. Jesus was causing them a lot of trouble and must be arrested and killed before he could cause more trouble. But how? The people would riot if they arrested him in public. Somehow it must be done secretly. They might need help.

But there are no secrets hidden from Jesus. He knew what was in their hearts and where his words and actions must lead him. He knew exactly where he was going and he was ahead of them all the way.

A jar of perfume
Mark 14:3-9

'Now, I assure you that wherever the gospel is preached all over the world, what she has done will be told in memory of her.' (Verse 9)

We're all different. Some of us are practical and tidy-minded—others are a bit harum-scarum. Some people look at a thing and think, 'How much did it cost?'—others think, 'What use is it?' and still others, 'It's very beautiful.' And sometimes, because we don't fully understand, we think that what somebody else has just done is silly.

Three hundred silver coins! Almost a wage for a whole year in those days. But the woman was guided by her heart, not her head. When she poured the perfume over Jesus she was showing her love for him, almost as if she knew what would happen to him very soon. She did a very special thing.

But Judas and some of those watching didn't understand. They looked at the perfume and just saw money, which was not its true value at all.

Jesus is sold
Mark 14:10-11

They were pleased to hear what he had to say, and promised to give him money. So Judas started looking for a good chance to hand Jesus over to them. (Verse 11)

Judas was disappointed. He was also greedy and selfish. He'd expected Jesus to be a rip-roaring conquering soldier, who would get rid of the Romans and give him and the other disciples important jobs and lots of money.

Instead, here was Jesus encouraging people to do silly things with expensive perfume and meekly talking about being killed. It didn't make sense.

So Judas offered his services to the priests and teachers—the side that looked like winning!

He was just the man they'd been looking for. They could arrest Jesus, in secret, now—before he caused more trouble for them. Judas could hand Jesus over to them... sell Jesus to them. And they would pay well for him!

So Judas lit the 'fuse'. The 'firework' that would set the world alight was ready to explode.

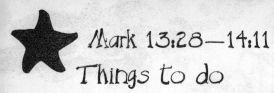

Mark 13:28—14:11

Things to do

Showing Jesus' love

Like the woman with the perfume, we can show Jesus our love for him. Fold a piece of A4 paper in half and cut it out in a nice perfume-bottle shape, making sure you leave a 'hinge' on the folded edge. Open it out and write inside a few ideas of things you could do to help someone. (Think of things that might cost you something, not in money, but perhaps in making you give up something else you wanted to do.) Do the things you thought of—just to show Jesus that you love him.

Toby + Trish — Show me

How do you make a granny knot?

Well, you make a loop, then...

Don't just tell me—
show me

The room is ready
Mark 14:12-16

The disciples left, went to the city, and found everything just as Jesus had told them; and they prepared the Passover meal. (Verse 16)

If you're having a party, preparing for it is almost as much fun as the party itself. There are invitations to send out, balloons to blow up, games to plan... and then there's the food. You want everything to be right because a party is a celebration.

The Passover was a celebration—and still is today. Everything had to be just right. For this particular Passover meal with Jesus, nothing must be allowed to happen that wasn't planned. Jesus himself had organized the room beforehand. The man with the jar of water met the disciples as planned. He led them to the owner of the house who showed them the room, all prepared, as planned. Everything had to be done in secret. Everything had gone according to plan. The room was ready for the most important celebration of all time.

A supper to remember
Mark 14:17-26

While they were eating, Jesus took a piece of bread, gave a prayer of thanks, broke it, and gave it to his disciples. 'Take it,' he said, 'this is my body.' (Verse 22)

'I've got a terrible memory,' you hear people say—perhaps you say it yourself. But we can usually remember what's important to us. In fact, memory itself is important to us! Sometimes a friend does something, or says something, or even wears something, and it reminds us of another time, perhaps another person.

At the Passover supper Jesus took the bread in his hands and broke it. Nothing unusual in that. The disciples had seen him do it hundreds of times before. Bread was an ordinary food, broken and eaten at every meal. But then... this time... 'This is my body,' Jesus said.

Because Jesus was important to them, the disciples would remember what he had said and what happened afterwards every time they themselves broke bread for a meal.

Lord Jesus, please be so important to me that I will always remember that you are with me. Amen

Crowing in the dark
Mark 14:27-31

Peter answered, 'I will never leave you, even though all the rest do!' Jesus said to Peter, 'I tell you that before the cock crows twice tonight, you will say three times that you do not know me.' (Verses 29–30)

Sometimes, with the best will in the world, we don't always manage to do what we say we'll do... tidy our room, feed the rabbit, write a 'thank you' letter... there's more! At the time we really mean what we say, then something else crops up and—ah well!

Peter loved Jesus and honestly believed that nothing—nothing—would ever make him pretend he didn't know him. It was unthinkable. Jesus loved Peter, and knew the terrible things that he would have to face—that they would all have to face. He was trying to warn him, to make him strong, so that when the time came he would be up to it. He even tried to soften the blow by promising to wait for them in Galilee—afterwards.

Agony in the garden
Mark 14:32-42

'Father,' Jesus prayed, 'my Father!
All things are possible for you. Take this cup
of suffering away from me. Yet not what I
want, but what you want.' (Verse 36)

There is a story about a little man who was very humble and had given everything he had to God. Suddenly he found that he wanted something from God—not for himself, but for someone else. He prayed, 'O Lord, for once—not what you want, but what I want!'

We all feel like that sometimes, wanting God to give us what *we* want. We would much rather have things our way than God's way.

In that beautiful garden, Jesus, deeply troubled, threw himself on the ground. He knew he was about to go through unbearable pain and sadness. He knew that his Father God was very close to him and could save him from all this. But he also knew that the pain and the sadness were the only way. So he bravely bowed his head to what God wanted.

...and he was one of his disciples

A single kiss
Mark 14:43-46

The traitor had given the crowd a signal: 'The man I kiss is the one you want. Arrest him and take him away under guard.' (Verse 44)

Sometimes when you're walking across the moors you see a sign: DANGER. DEEP BOG. KEEP OFF. So, of course, you don't go anywhere near that bit because you know that if you did you would sink. You wouldn't be able to get out in time and gradually the bog would pull you under.

Wanting to do what we know to be wrong is like that—only often there's no warning 'DANGER' sign. Judas was so caught up with his own selfish plans that he had stepped off the path, without even noticing the warning sign.

He called Jesus 'Teacher', someone who is respected, and he kissed him—a sign of love. Judas no longer knew, or cared, what respect and love meant. He had sunk so low that the 'bog' had pulled him under.

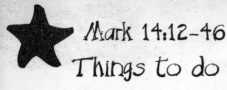

Mark 14:12-46
Things to do

Countdown

Before Jesus left the garden, it was all systems go for the most amazing event in the history of the world. Make a clock for the countdown and attach a pointer with a split-pin paper-fastener so that you can move it on as the story continues.

Toby + Trish — Quick snack

10, 9, 8, 7, 6, 5, 4, 3, 2, 1

Boomerang's finished his tea!

I'm like that whenever I wake up!

Running away
Mark 14:47-51

Then all the disciples left him and ran away. (Verse 50)

Have you ever been woken up in the middle of the night by someone who wants you to do something? For a minute you can't think who or where you are. You're totally useless.

Jesus had asked the disciples to stay awake—three times. He needed them. But it was late. They were tired. They fell asleep.

If they hadn't fallen asleep they might have been more use to Jesus when he was arrested. Instead they were totally useless. They ran away.

Some people think that the young man who had been following Jesus and also ran away was Mark himself. It was a night he would never forget!

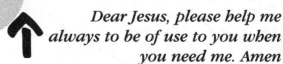

Dear Jesus, please help me always to be of use to you when you need me. Amen

91

Warm but not comfortable
Mark 14:53-54

Peter followed from a distance, and went into the courtyard of the High Priest's house. There he sat down with the guards, keeping himself warm by the fire. (Verse 54)

If we think we stick out like a sore thumb and everybody's looking at us, we feel uncomfortable. Maybe that's why we wear similar clothes to our friends—trainers, jeans, baseball caps, T-shirts. We're usually happier if we're one of the crowd.

Peter definitely wanted to be one of the crowd. He dreaded being noticed. As it was the middle of the night, everyone was gathered around the fires in the courtyard. So there Peter huddled, torn apart by his thoughts... he hated himself... he too could be arrested... he had let Jesus down... what would happen to Jesus now?

After Jesus was arrested, Peter had followed behind as closely as he dared. He couldn't bear not to be with Jesus now. So there he sat, warm and cosy on the outside, but cold with fear and despair on the inside.

I think the chief priests were on trial

An unfair trial
Mark 14:55-65

The chief priests and the whole Council tried to find some evidence against Jesus in order to put him to death, but they could not find any. (Verse 55)

Trials are usually very serious affairs where everything is done properly. Deciding whether a person is innocent or guilty of a crime is an important matter.

Jesus' trial was nothing like that. To begin with, the whole thing was illegal because the Council weren't allowed to meet at night. But the priests didn't dare wait—they had to be rid of Jesus, at all costs. Also, they'd decided Jesus was guilty even before the trial began. The trouble was that they weren't sure what he *had* done. Then, because of the rush there'd been no time to tell the 'witnesses' how to lie, so their stories didn't match.

Hatred, jealousy, greed, ambition, lies, anger—every sort of badness was there that night. But perfect goodness was there too. Jesus stood calmly, quite alone, in the middle of it all—and waited.

Who?!

Mark 14:66-72

Just then a cock crowed a second time, and Peter remembered how Jesus had said to him, 'Before the cock crows twice, you will say three times that you do not know me.' And he broke down and cried. (Verse 72)

We've thought in some of the other readings about how a certain thing happening can take us back to a different time and place.

A cock crowing is not unusual towards dawn. The first time it crowed Peter was so unhappy he scarcely heard it. The second time the full meaning hit him— hard. He was taken back to another place, the Mount of Olives, when they were all together with Jesus. He heard the voice of Jesus—read it again for yourself in chapter 14 verse 30. And, just as important, he heard his own voice, his own reply—read that again in verse 31.

To Peter, the dreadful events seemed to have gone on for ever. Yet they had been on the Mount of Olives only a few hours before. 'What have I done?' Peter, who had been braver than most, cried bitterly.

But Jesus forgave Peter—and later he became a great man.

Is Jesus going to be freed?

Pilate's problem
Mark 15:1-10

*Pilate asked them,
'Do you want me to set free for you
the king of the Jews?' (Verse 9)*

Pilate was the Roman governor and he was feeling fed up. He'd left his comfortable seaside villa in Caesarea and come to noisy, crowded Jerusalem to keep the peace at Passover time. These Jewish priests with another of their everlasting religious squabbles were the last straw.

But when Pilate came face to face with Jesus he was amazed. This man was different. How could he sentence an obviously innocent man to death? Even if he were the king of the Jews, he seemed to be no threat to the Roman Empire.

Pilate had a problem on his hands. He didn't want to risk trouble with the priests—or with the people, who would surely want their king released. What to do? Then he had an idea.

It was a Passover custom to release a prisoner. He'd questioned Jesus, as the priests demanded; now he could release him at the people's request. That would be an end to the matter... or so he thought!

Mark 14:47—15:10

Things to do

Missing persons

Fold a piece of A4 paper in half and draw Jesus on one side all by himself. Then draw a large crowd on the other side and make a list of all his friends, whom we have read about over the last few weeks. Where were they?

Toby+Trish | Missing

Where were you when they were asking for volunteers for the sponsored walk?

I was on an unsponsored walk to the sweet shop

To please the crowd
Mark 15:11-15

Pilate wanted to please the crowd, so he set Barabbas free for them. Then he had Jesus whipped and handed him over to be crucified. (Verse 15)

'Barabbas!' Pilate couldn't believe his ears. 'Barabbas!' The last name Pilate wanted to hear. Barabbas was a terrorist, leader of a riot against the Romans. And what about 'the king of the Jews'?

The priests had done their work well. An excited crowd is easy to persuade. They thought Jesus had let them down—Barabbas at least had been willing to fight for his country.

'Barabbas!' Louder and louder. Pilate's job was to keep the peace, at any price. So he released Barabbas, a terrorist, and sent Jesus, an innocent man, to his death.

Pilate knew what was right, but he wasn't strong enough to do it. He let himself be influenced by those who shouted the loudest.

Jesus, please make me strong to do what is right, no matter what people are saying. Amen

The purple robe
Mark 15:16-20

They put a purple robe on Jesus,
made a crown out of thorny branches,
and put it on his head. (Verse 17)

Different colours mean different things to us. Blue reminds us of the sea and makes us feel cool; green is like walking in the country—it's restful. Yellow is like... what do you think?

Not long ago only kings wore purple. Today, although anybody can wear it, it's still a 'royal' colour.

But the purple robe that they put on Jesus was a fake—a 'pretend' kingly garment. It was probably a soldier's old faded red cloak that looked purple in the blue shadows of the courtyard.

The crown too was a fake—a cruel joke. Everything in that courtyard was a fake. But for one thing!

Jesus. He was what he said he was: the real and true Son of God. King, not just of the Jews, but of the whole world.

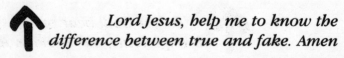

Lord Jesus, help me to know the difference between true and fake. Amen

'Through'
Mark 15:21-32

It was nine o'clock in the morning when they crucified him. (Verse 25)

There is a famous picture owned by an army regiment called *The Royal Signals*. In times of war their job is to get messages through from the fighting back to headquarters. Very important! Why?

The picture is called *Through*. It shows a brave soldier who has been shot whilst trying to mend a break in a signal wire. No messages could get through. But before he died he managed to grasp both ends of the wire in his outstretched hand. The messages could actually go *through* his body, from the fighting to the headquarters.

When Jesus died on the cross his outstretched arms reconnected us to God, our 'headquarters'. The things we do wrong cut us off from God, but Jesus has mended the break in the wire with his own body. We can now get *through* to our heavenly Father.

Father God, hear our prayers, through Jesus, our Saviour. Amen

98

Good Friday is 'God's Friday'

The curtain tears in two
Mark 15:33-39

The curtain hanging in the Temple was torn in two, from top to bottom. (Verse 38)

Where I used to go for my holidays there was a house we called 'the sad house'. Can you guess why? For some reason the curtains were always drawn across every window, just as though it was cut off from everything and everybody. Imagine the rooms—no daylight, no life.

The curtain of the temple was drawn across the entrance to the most sacred part of the temple: the Holy of Holies. The Jewish people believed that God was there in a special way. There were no windows, no daylight. It was shut off from everything and everybody except the High Priest, who went in once a year.

When Jesus died on the cross, this curtain was torn in two. Daylight flooded in. It was a sign, like the one we thought about yesterday, that the way to God was open. For all of us. *Through* Jesus.

A very large stone
Mark 15:42-47

Joseph bought a linen sheet, took the body down, wrapped it in the sheet, and placed it in a tomb which had been dug out of solid rock. Then he rolled a large stone across the entrance to the tomb. (Verse 46)

Why is it that we're always trying to shut God up in small places? Maybe in a church—yesterday we thought about the Holy of Holies—and now today...

Have you ever tried to lift an enormous pebble—the biggest on the beach? Big enough to sit on! It's amazing how heavy it is. Now think of it maybe three hundred times bigger... and heavier. And keep on thinking!

The tomb that Joseph gave had been prepared for himself—out of solid rock. Nothing could get in except through the opening.

Ready? Joseph would have needed lots of help to move that stone you're thinking about, until it completely blocked the entrance to the tomb. It was a *very large stone*.

And, once in place, it looked as if it was there for good. End of story?

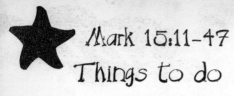

Mark 15:11-47

Things to do

...were you there?

There is an old song that asks, 'Were you there when they crucified my Lord?' The answer is yes —we were all there because, before he died, Jesus took upon himself all the things we do wrong. He paid the price for us. For Jesus the awfulness of the cross was the gateway to our happiness—that's why we use it as a symbol of his love. Cut a cross out of card, as in the picture, and then look through magazines for beautiful, joyful coloured pictures— holidays, flowers, smiling faces—and stick them in a collage all over the cross. Put the cross on your bedroom wall.

You weren't there

I thought Mum would be cross with me for dropping the milk bottle on the kitchen floor...

It's all right—you weren't there so I said it was me

Whatever's going to happen next?
Mark 16:1-4

On the way the women said to one another,
'Who will roll away the stone for us from the
entrance to the tomb?' (It was a very large stone.)
Then they looked up and saw that the stone had
already been rolled back. (Verses 3–4)

Sometimes a lot of unpleasant things happen to us, one after the other. Maybe we lose something we like, then we catch a nasty cold, then a favourite teacher leaves, then our pet dies. Oh dear! It's a bad time. 'Whatever's going to happen next?'

Jesus' friends and disciples had had a bad time. They'd seen Jesus suffer and die on the cross... Jesus, whom they loved. And there'd been nothing they could do. They felt lost—their world had fallen apart—and afraid in case the soldiers came to arrest them. 'Whatever's going to happen next?'

As the women, worn out with crying, approached the tomb, they saw that the very large stone had been rolled away. Somebody had been there before them. What had happened to the body of Jesus? Oh dear! 'Whatever's going to happen next?'

1Ø1

Hooray for Easter Day!

The impossible has happened!
Mark 16:5-8

'Don't be alarmed,' he said. 'I know you are looking for Jesus of Nazareth, who was crucified. He is not here—he has been raised! Look, here is the place where they put him.' (Verse 6)

Yesterday we thought about bad times. Everybody has them—you, me, the disciples. The trouble is that when this happens we begin to *expect* things to go wrong. We *expect* the worst, so that when the best happens we can hardly realize it.

The women didn't realize that the stone was rolled away especially for *them*—so that they could see with their own eyes that the body of Jesus had gone. They didn't realize that the young man in white was waiting especially for *them*—to explain what had happened.

They had forgotten Jesus' promise to meet them in Galilee after the crucifixion. How could they go back and tell what they'd just seen and heard? It was impossible.

Because of their own fears, they didn't realize that the impossible had happened. *Jesus was alive!*

 Lord Jesus, help us not to miss your blessings because of our own fears. Amen

Then they believed
Mark 16:9-14

Last of all, Jesus appeared to the eleven disciples as they were eating. He scolded them, because they did not have faith and because they were too stubborn to believe those who had seen him alive.
(Verse 14)

In a few short minutes the lives of the disciples were changed.

They'd been frightened, sad, ashamed, confused. There had been so many rumours about what had happened to Jesus. Some people actually said they'd seen him alive. How could they believe that? All the teaching they'd had from Jesus, all their faith, had drained away.

Then Jesus came to them. Then they believed.

He'd promised to meet them in Galilee, but because of how they were feeling, he came to them earlier, in Jerusalem. And because they wouldn't believe what had happened, and because he loved them, he gave them a good telling-off!

 Jesus, please help me to believe so that my life is changed. Amen

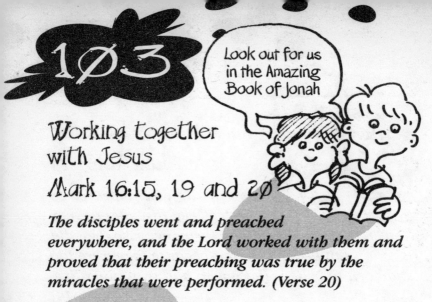

10.3

Look out for us in the Amazing Book of Jonah

Working together with Jesus
Mark 16:15, 19 and 20

The disciples went and preached everywhere, and the Lord worked with them and proved that their preaching was true by the miracles that were performed. (Verse 20)

Just imagine you've been told some really exciting news. The sort of news that makes you want to jump up and down and shout. You couldn't just keep it to yourself, could you? You'd want to share it—so that other people could feel like you do.

The disciples had no doubts now that Jesus was alive again. How could they keep this good news to themselves? Jesus had told them to share it with everybody—and they couldn't wait to get started. The wonder was, they knew he would be caring and sharing in whatever they were doing.

We've read Mark's amazing book. We've heard the best news there ever was. Jesus is alive! How can we keep it to ourselves? Let's share it! And the wonder is—Jesus is with us whatever we're doing. This good news can change the world!

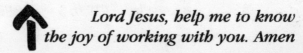

Lord Jesus, help me to know the joy of working with you. Amen